Are You Happy?

AND OTHER QUESTIONS LOVERS ASK

EDWARD KOREN

Pantheon Books, New York

To Jane

All rights reserved under International and Pan-American Copy-
right Conventions. Published in the United States by Pantheon
Books, a division of Random House, Inc., New York, and simulta-
neously in Canada by Random House of Canada Limited, Toronto.
The drawings on pages 9, 13, 18, 19, 26, 41, 42, 44, and 48 appeared
originally in *The New Yorker* and were Copyrighted © 1978 by
The New Yorker Magazine, Inc.

Library of Congress Cataloging in Publication Data

Koren, Edward.
  Are You Happy?

    Cartoons.
    1. American wit and humor, Pictorial.   I.   Title.
NC1429.K62A4   1978   741.5'973   78-53922
ISBN 0-394-50271-X

Manufactured in the United States of America

  4689753

"What do you do? Where did you grow up? Where do you live? How long were you married? Are you going with anyone special? May I see you again?"

"Don't you want to know everything about me?"

"Underneath it all, what are you really like?"

"You must be terribly hurt."

"Have you always stayed friends with your former lovers?"

"Has it ever been like this for you before?"

"What are you like when you get angry?"

"What are you thinking about?"

"*Tell me about your first husband.*"

"Do you know what *a* supportive person you are?"

"Don't you love being spontaneous?"

"Are you frightened?"

"Was that good for you?"

"We've been together three weeks? Has it really been that long?"

"Do we have to analyze everything?"

"How can someone as wonderful as you not like yourself?"

"Do I satisfy your needs?"

"Is there something you'd like me to do?"

"Do you think I'm attractive?"

"Why do we always see your friends?"

"Why do your plans always leave me out?"

"Are you trying to pressure me?"

"I'm tired of talking for both of us. Will you please say something?"

"Why can't you accept intimacy?"

"Do you have to chew your food like that?"

"Why don't you ever say you love me?"

"Why does your life have to begin and end with me?"

"Are you doing this because you feel guilty?"

"Are you going to <u>just</u> go to sleep?"

"What do you mean, I'm just like your ex-wife?"

"Don't you like to touch me any more?"

"How can I love someone who doesn't like my cats?"

"Have you been seeing someone else?"

"What have I done to make you so angry?"

"*Why do you always make me feel foolish and stupid?*"

"Where <u>were</u> you all day?"

"*Don't you realize how angry you are at women?*"

"What right have you to speak to me that way?"

"Why is your work *always* more important than our relationship?"

"Don't you think you should be getting professional help?"

"Can't we talk about anything except 'us'?"

"*What is it you want—just tell me—what is it you want?*"

"Why is it always <u>my</u> fault?"

"Darling, can't we give it one more try?"

"Didn't I tell you I never wanted to see you again?"

"Do you think we could stay friends?"